OAKWOOD SCHOOL
255 CLARENCE AVENUE
PORT COLBORNE, ONT.

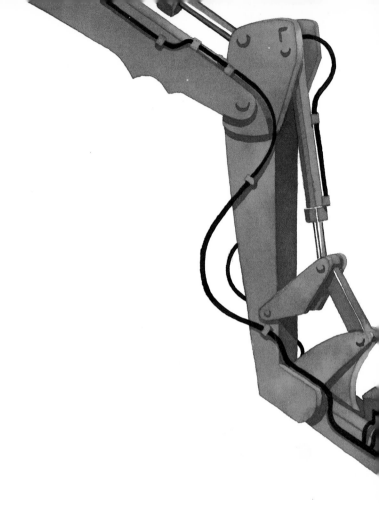

Copyright © 1989 Paul Stickland
Printed by permission of Mathew Price Ltd., England
First Canadian edition published 1989

Canadian Cataloguing in Publication Data

Stickland, Paul
  Machines as big as monsters

ISBN 0-921103-72-7
1. Machinery – Juvenile literature. . I. Title.

TJ147.S84 1989·ʸ   j621.8   C88-094993-7

Kids Can Press Ltd.
585½ Bloor Street West
Toronto, Ontario, Canada   M6G 1K5

Designed by Herman Lelie
Printed in Italy for Imago

89 0 9 8 7 6 5 4 3 2 1

MACHINES
AS BIG AS
MONSTERS

PAUL STICKLAND

Kids Can Press

The Terex Titan is the largest dump truck in the world. It has a huge diesel engine which powers electric motors for each of its 10 wheels, and it can carry up to 350 tonnes at a time. This one is taking copper ore from the quarry to the factory.

This monstrous floating crane is lowering the platform of an oil rig precisely into place. It is being steered by two tugs, and also by its own propellors. Besides building works it is also used for rescuing sunken ships.

A walking dragline excavator rumbles slowly along on caterpillar tracks. This one is digging out huge mouthfuls of sand in a bucket big enough to hold a bulldozer. It is cutting a canal through the desert to bring water to the dry lands.

OAKWOOD SCHOOL
255 OMER AVENUE
PORT COLBORNE, ONT.

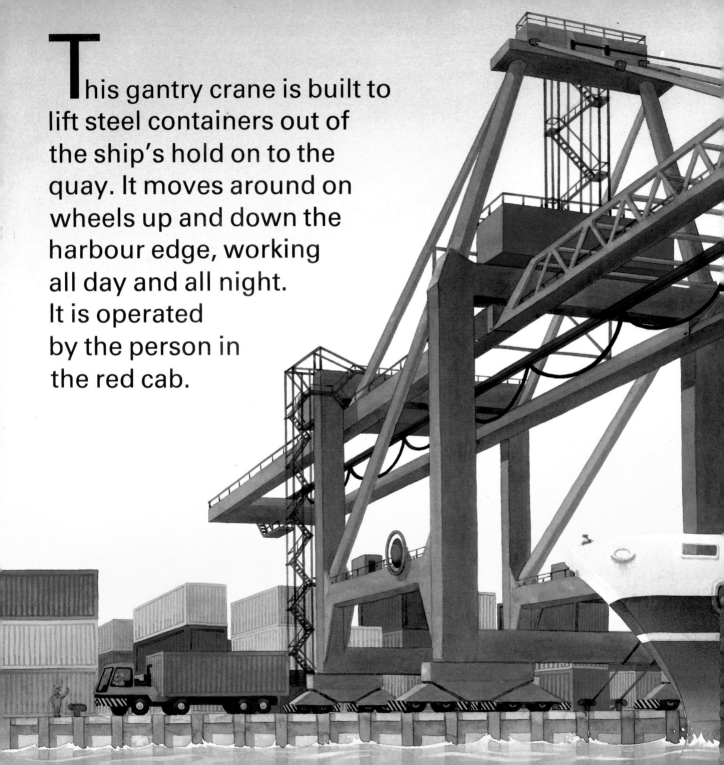

This gantry crane is built to lift steel containers out of the ship's hold on to the quay. It moves around on wheels up and down the harbour edge, working all day and all night. It is operated by the person in the red cab.

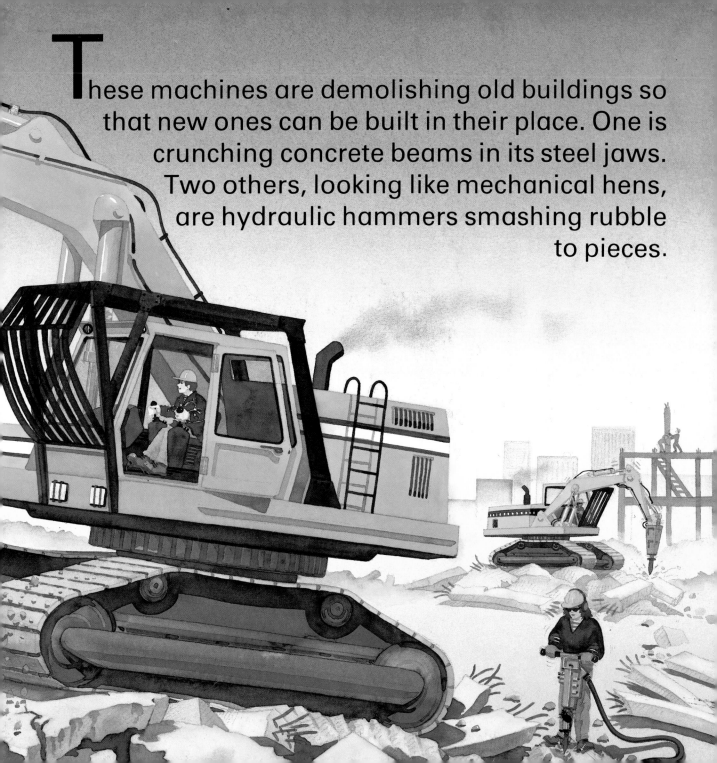

These machines are demolishing old buildings so that new ones can be built in their place. One is crunching concrete beams in its steel jaws. Two others, looking like mechanical hens, are hydraulic hammers smashing rubble to pieces.

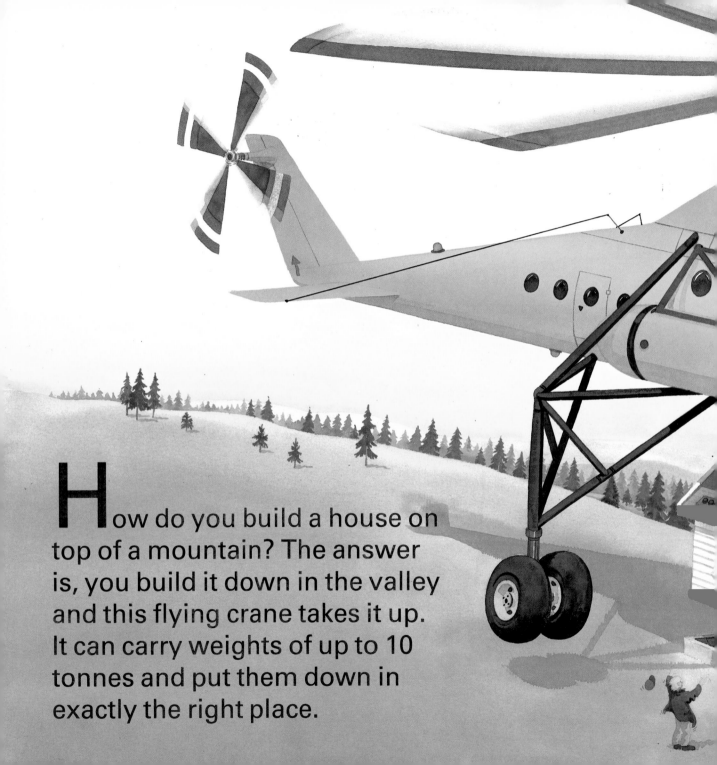

How do you build a house on top of a mountain? The answer is, you build it down in the valley and this flying crane takes it up. It can carry weights of up to 10 tonnes and put them down in exactly the right place.

The Galaxy C5 is the largest aircraft in the world. When it is ready to load, it sinks down on to its 28 gigantic wheels, its nose comes up and its ramp comes down, just like a huge mouth opening. This one is loading 16 trucks, each weighing three-quarters of a tonne. When they are all inside and its giant mouth is shut, it will rise up on its wheels again and take off into the sky.

This Skylab space station was the first one to be lived in by astronauts. It circled the earth, far out in space where there is no air and no gravity. Three teams of three astronauts were brought up and back by rockets.

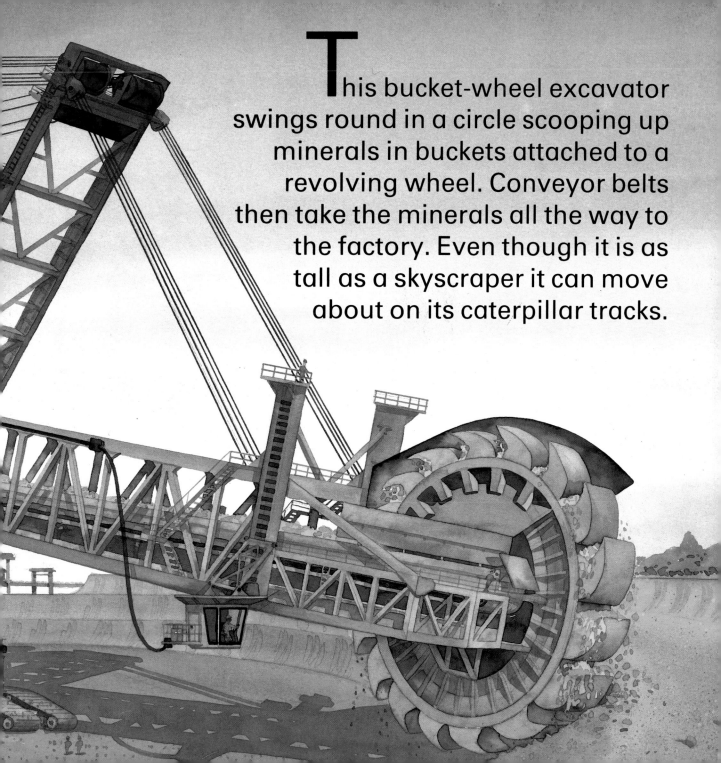

This bucket-wheel excavator swings round in a circle scooping up minerals in buckets attached to a revolving wheel. Conveyor belts then take the minerals all the way to the factory. Even though it is as tall as a skyscraper it can move about on its caterpillar tracks.

The Thames barrier is a dam built to protect London from surge tides. Freak storms could cause the river to flood and devastate the city. Each gate lies flat on the river bed until it is needed. Then wheels at either side move it into the upright position. The red crosses and green arrows tell ships which gates are open.

The chain bucket dredger is making deep water for ships to sail through. It scoops up soft sand and mud from the harbour floor and pours it into the barge standing by. This will then take it out to sea and dump it – or even make little islands out of it.

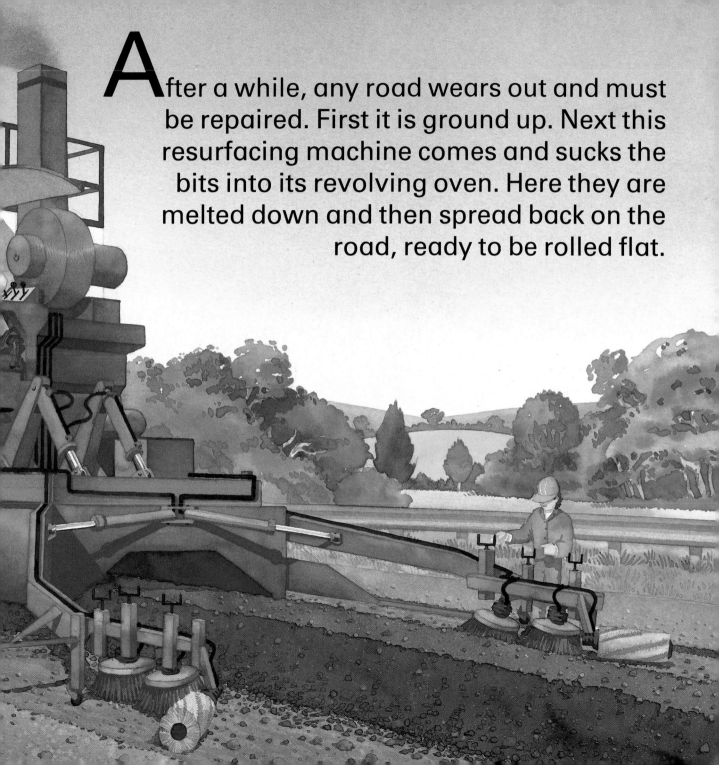

After a while, any road wears out and must be repaired. First it is ground up. Next this resurfacing machine comes and sucks the bits into its revolving oven. Here they are melted down and then spread back on the road, ready to be rolled flat.

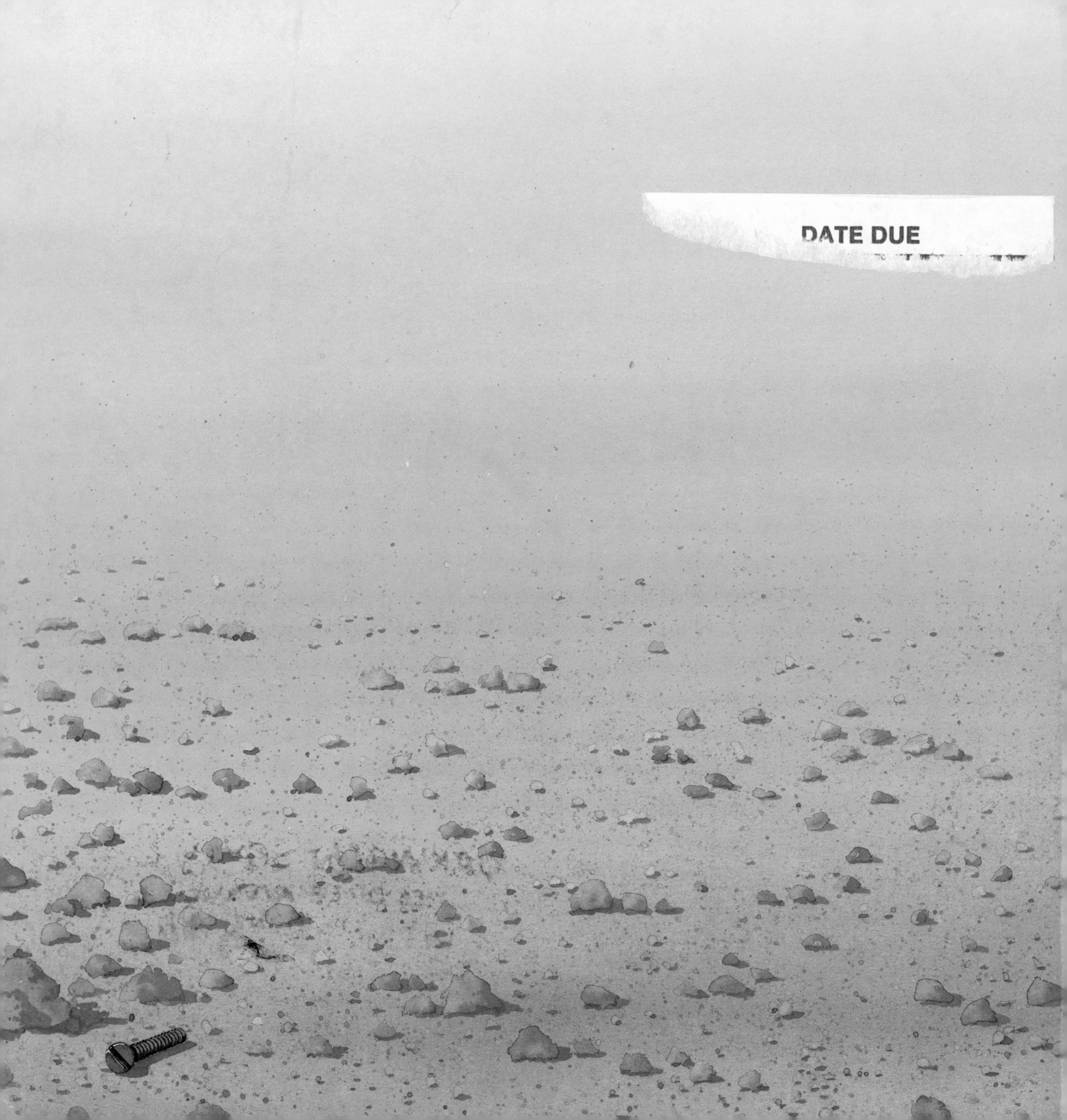